DATE DUE			
MAR 17 '98			
APR 1 '98			
NOV 18 '00			
JAN 03 '01			
JUN 28 '04			
AUG 1 0 09			
NO 0 8 '10			
AUG 7 2015			

I want to be

A PUPPETEER

Ivan Bulloch & Diane James

STARRING

TOM

CARLI

JASON

NICOLE

LIZZIE

JORDAN

WORLD BOOK
In association with
TWO-CAN

Photography © Fiona Pragoff
Illustrations Debi Ani
Design Assistant Lisa Nutt

First published in the United States in 1996 by
World Book, Inc., 525 W. Monroe, 20th Floor, Chicago, IL USA 60661
in association with Two-Can Publishing Ltd.

Copyright © Two-Can Publishing Ltd., 1996

**For information on other World Book products,
call 1-800-255-1750, x 2238.**

ISBN: 0-7166-1744-7 (pbk.)
ISBN: 0-7166-1743-9 (hbk.)
LC: 96-60463

791.5

Printed in Hong Kong

1 2 3 4 5 6 7 8 9 10 99 98 97 96

CONTENTS

I WANT TO BE A PUPPETEER

As a puppeteer you will certainly be busy. There are puppets to make, stages to build, scenery and props to gather, and lots of practicing to do. You will have to get to know your puppets well. The puppeteer has to control the puppets and bring them alive! There are lots of different kinds of puppets, and by the end of this book you will have met all of them!

Put on a shadow puppet show for your friends.

Find out how to make all sorts of puppets, including string puppets.

Finger puppets are great for an instant performance.

Discover how to bring a dust mop alive!

The puppeteer has to turn a puppet into a character through the way the puppet moves or speaks.

FINGER PUPPETS

This is a great way to start puppeteering because you can have puppets at your fingertips almost instantly!

Hair-raiser!

Roll up a tube of construction or tissue paper and fringe one end. Poke the tube into the top of your finger puppet for a good head of hair. Or make two slits opposite each other in the tube and slot a hairstyle in—like the one opposite!

Choose a character first, then give it a face.

Shredded paper makes great hair for a cheerful finger puppet.

Body tube

Cut a strip of paper wide enough to fit the top of your finger above the knuckle. It should be long enough to wrap around your finger and be taped together. Cut a face shape from a piece of paper or thin cardboard. You can either draw the features on or cut shapes from colored paper and glue them on. When you are happy with the face, glue it to the body tube.

You guessed right! I'm Mr. Happy!

Wiggle your finger to make the puppet move.

It's amazing how much a different hairstyle can change the look of a puppet!

Who am I?

When you are acting you can change your expression, move around, and make gestures with your arms. Puppets depend on the puppeteer to bring them to life. You can make them move, make them talk, and with some puppets—such as the sock puppets on the next page—you can even change their expressions.

Try to keep the puppets facing the audience.

Don't call me big nose!

SOCK OR GLOVE?

Here's a challenge! How can you turn a sock and two washcloths into a couple of smart-aleck puppets?

Bzzzzzzz! That looks like a good flower!

Very handy
Puppets that fit on your hand are called glove puppets. Some have a head and arms that you operate with your fingers. Others, like the ones here, are simpler, but they still have loads of character.

Look for styrofoam balls in craft shops. They are very light and make excellent eyes. Paint them and glue them to your puppets.

Sew loops of yarn through the top of the sock for hair.

Super socks
You can turn a sock into a puppet instantly without adding anything at all, but eyes and hair help to give it personality. Put your thumb in the heel and the rest of your fingers in the toe of the sock.

Sew what!

Put your hand on a piece of paper—fingers together—and draw around it. Use this shape as a pattern and cut out two pieces of fabric. We used two washcloths, but you could use felt or any material that doesn't fray. Put one piece on top of the other and start sewing around the outside.

He looks like something I wash my face with!

Buttons make good eyes, too!

Hands in!

Put your whole hand inside and see what you can do to move the puppet around.

That's weird, that striped guy looks just like a sock!

When you get near the top of the head, lay some short pieces of yarn between the two cloths. Keep stitching and you'll trap the yarn and give your puppet a head of hair! Glue on two styrofoam balls for eyes and a long piece of yarn to make a combined mouth and nose.

To make a sad puppet, just turn the mouth down.

TWIST AND TURN

Here is another kind of puppet that is easy to make and to operate. All the puppets here are called rod or stick puppets. The rod acts as the back for the puppet and moves the puppet around.

It's up to you!

Good organization and lots of practice are vital before you put on a show. You may be the only puppeteer and have a large cast of puppets to deal with!

I'm so sorry— you look like a friend of mine!

Good! The disguise worked. I don't think she's recognized me!

Mop it up!

String or sponge mops can become puppets within seconds. They just need to be clean and to have a clever puppeteer to bring them to life.

Add a nose and two ribbons to a dust mop to make a cute dog.

Sponge man

All sorts of things may come in handy for making rod puppets, so keep a collection of odds and ends. Gardening stakes and dowels from hardware stores make good rods.

To make a rod puppet like the one on this page, you'll need a rod, an empty round box for the head, a small cardboard tube (cut in half) for the arms, some colored paper, and, of course, a sponge! Paint the box and the tube before you stick your puppet together with strong glue.

Hats on!

Cut a circle of paper about 6 inches across. Then cut out a wedge. Make a cone and tape it. Thread a piece of elastic—long enough to fit around the box—into each side of the cone.

Cut some funny shaped hands from paper. Cut slits and slot them onto the ends of the tube.

Use a pair of scissors to make a slit in the sponge. Push the rod into the slit.

ARMS AND LEGS

So far the puppets we've used have not been able to move about much. But these rod puppets are a little looser!

Paint all the pieces before you put them together. Don't tie the hands and arms too tightly, or they will not be able to move. Allow a little slack. Now try your puppet out! By twisting the rod in your hand, you'll be able to make the puppet swing its arms. Try this slowly, then very quickly.

Cardboard tubes for arms

Cardboard box with one end open

Make a hole in the sponge hands. Knot the end of the cord.

Sponge head
Make a hole in the closed end of the box for the rod and make a hole on each side for a piece of thick cord to thread through. Use the picture as a guide to make the puppet's hands and arms.

Hey! Watch me move!

Use one rod to move the arm and the other to move the puppet.

Shake hands!

Some rod puppets are made with two rods. The second rod operates one of the arms. This gives you more control over what your puppet can do.

Make the rods long enough so your hands will not show when you are performing.

Draw a character on cardboard. Cut off one of the arms and use it as a pattern to make a slightly longer one. Attach the moving arm to the body with a paper fastener. Thread a piece of string through the arm and knot it. Tie the other end to one of the rods. Glue the second rod to the back of the puppet.

STAGESTRUCK!

After you've practiced different ways to make your puppets move, you'll be ready to try them out on a stage. Think about backgrounds, sound effects, and good story lines.

When you are making your theater, keep in mind the size of your puppets!

From the bottom

All the puppets we've looked at so far are worked from below the stage and held above the puppeteer. This means you'll need a stage that hides your body and is big enough for you to move around in comfortably.

We made our stage from two cardboard boxes. The big one came from a store that sells washing machines and refrigerators. Cut a panel in one of the sides of the big box so you can get in and out. Cut another panel in the top. With the small box you'll need to cut three panels—one for the front so the audience can see, one on the bottom for the puppets to come through, and one on top for the backdrop.

Depending on the size of the box, you can either kneel or stand.

Bring the play to life with a background scene.

14

Decorate the boxes and glue them together with strong glue. Attach a piece of fabric at the side so the audience cannot see you. Paint a backdrop on a separate piece of paper, or make a paper collage. Glue the backdrop to a dowel and balance it on top of the stage. Take your puppets inside and practice moving around in there!

It's great being a puppet. You never get nervous in front of an audience!

If possible, make a small shelf inside your theater to hold puppets that are not onstage.

It's a little tight with two of us in here, but we'll manage!

Cut shapes from cardboard. Paint them and glue them to your theater.

Get a partner to help so you can see what the puppets look like from the front.

TIPS

★ **Large cardboard boxes are not easy to find! Ask local storekeepers to save a few for you.**
★ **Look for our ideas later on for making "instant" theaters.**

SHADOWS

Shadow puppets are among the oldest puppets in the world. You'll need a special stage to show your puppets and a light source, which you can find out about on page 18.

Make your puppets move with the help of a paper fastener and an extra rod.

The plot comes first

As with all puppetry, it's important that you get your ideas, plot, and characters figured out first. Then the puppet making will be easy!

He looks mighty fierce! Better steer clear!

Shadow puppets are most effective if they are black on the front.

Through a screen

Shadow puppets are different from the other puppets we've looked at because the audience sees them through a screen. The shadows that appear on the front of the screen look mysterious. The puppets are operated close to the back of the screen, so it is best to attach the rods to the backs of them at right angles.

Cut them out

Draw the outline shapes of your puppets on cardboard and cut them out. It can be quite effective if you cut out small shapes from the main pieces.
If you are making a moving puppet, make sure you allow enough overlap on the separate pieces.

Practice in front of a mirror so you can see what your puppet is doing.

TIPS

★ Use thick cardboard for your puppets so that they stand up to the wear and tear of performing.
★ Make your rods more secure by sticking a thumbtack through the front of the puppet.

Make them work

For unjointed puppets, glue one rod to the back near the middle. For jointed puppets, make a hole in both pieces of cardboard where they overlap and push a paper fastener through. Glue one rod to the main puppet part and the other to the part that moves.

LIGHTS UP!

As soon as you've figured out the plot and made your shadow puppets, you will need a theater and a source of light to put on a show.

Frame and screen
Choose a sturdy cardboard box—not too deep—that will stand on its side without wobbling. This will be your shadow theater.

Decorate
the outside of the box with paint, colored paper, and glitter for a sparkly effect. Prop your theater on a table and shine a heavy-duty flashlight on the back of the screen.

Cut out most of the bottom of the box, leaving a frame around the edges. Tape a sheet of strong tracing paper to the frame, as shown above.

Using daylight

A flashlight is fine for a small tabletop screen, but if your screen is larger you may need to rig up a lamp to give enough light. The stronger the light source, the clearer the shadows will be. Avoid using more than one light source because this will make your shadows appear blurred.

If you are putting on your show during the day, you'll probably find that ordinary daylight will give you enough light. Bright sunlight is best. Whatever the source of light, your puppets must be operated between it and the screen.

Keep the rest of your puppets out of the way so they don't make a shadow on the screen. But not too far away!

Hey, Max! Do you think you could teach me that dance?

PULL A STRING

String puppets are probably the most popular of all puppets. Unlike other puppets, they are operated from above. Some of them have lots of strings, but it's best to start with a simple one.

Curious bird
Both of these bouncy bird puppets were made from flat, round boxes. Look for three boxes or flat, round deli containers. The feet are pieces of sponge.

Open the box to thread the cord through.

Thread a piece of thick cord through one box to make legs. Then thread each end through a sponge foot. Knot the ends of the cord.

Make a beak by cutting a section from a round box. This is tricky, so ask an adult for help. Glue the beak to the smaller box, then glue the whole bird's head onto its body.

Paint the pieces before you put them together.

Crossbar and strings
String puppets are operated by moving strings that are attached to various parts of the puppet. The strings are tied to a crossbar. The puppeteer makes the puppet move by controlling the crossbar. You will see how this is done as soon as you try it. Make the crossbar from two strips of balsa wood. Wind string around the point where the pieces cross to keep them in place.

I should really try to keep out of the way!

I wonder when I get to fly!

The last step is to attach the strings to the bird and then to the crossbar. Thread a piece of string through each of the sponge feet and knot the ends so they don't slip through. Tape a third piece of string to the middle of the bird's back. Adjust the lengths of the strings and tie them to the crossbar using the drawing here as a guide.

Move each foot in turn by rocking the crossbar from side to side.

FOUR LEGS

Now that you know how string puppets work, try making one with four legs and a head that moves!

Leave the boxes open until you have added the strings.

Spotted cow

First, gather the things you need. We used cardboard boxes for the body, head, and feet. The legs and neck can be made from thick, colored shoelaces or cord.

Attach the head to the body with a piece of cord. Add a tail and you're nearly ready to add the strings! You'll need to make a crossbar from three pieces of wood. Tie the wood together by winding string where the pieces of wood join.

Paint the boxes first.

Make four holes in the sides of a large box and thread the cord through as shown. Then thread the cord through the small boxes. Knot the ends to keep the cords in place.

Ask an adult to help you make the holes.

This is more like it! I can chase the silly sheep now.

Use neutral-colored string so it doesn't stand out.

Try making other animals using the same method.

Adding the strings
Thread and knot pieces of string through each of the feet, next to the cord legs. You'll also need a string in the middle of the head and the middle of the body. Adjust the lengths and use the photograph above as a guide to tie the strings to the crossbar.

Off we go!
Now you can have some fun! Hold the long piece of the crossbar. By rocking it gently from side to side, make the cow lift each of its legs in turn. You can make him lie down, sit, and nod his head! What else can you do?

STRING SHOW

When you and your string puppets are ready to put on a show, you will need a different kind of stage because the puppets are operated from above.

I have the strangest feeling that I'm being followed!

Setting the scene

There are all kinds of ways to make stages for string puppets. We've chosen something very simple!

Start with the backdrop. Paint a scene on a large sheet of cardboard or paper, or make a collage using shapes cut from colored paper. If you use a paper background, glue it to cardboard to make it sturdy.

Make sure your backdrop will stand up on its own, leaving you free to operate the puppets. Cut two large right-angle triangles from thick cardboard. Score along one of the edges that forms the right angle and fold back a flap. Tape the flaps to the back of the backdrop.

Sometimes you'll need to change backdrops between scenes. Make the new backdrops from paper and then simply attach them to your original board with large binder clips. This should take only seconds!

Extra props

You may want to add a few extra props to your stage set to give it depth. Here's an easy way to make a tree. Cut two tree shapes from cardboard. In one of them, cut a slit from the top to the middle. In the other, cut a slit from the bottom to the middle. Slot them together and stand the tree up.

I can't believe I haven't been spotted yet!

For a large backdrop, use more than two triangles.

You can make all sorts of things using the slit-and-slot method.

IT'S BIG!

Here's a chance to turn yourself into a giant puppet and put on a really BIG show!

I could deal with someone pulling my strings!

Don't bend your arms or legs!

Put on the legs first, then the body, arms, and finally the head.

Robot tricks

Try to find some corrugated cardboard used for packing. It has ridges and bends easily. Otherwise, use thin cardboard. Ask a friend to measure you. Cut out tubes to fit around your head, body, arms, and legs. Cut out shapes in the head piece for your eyes and mouth, and cut two arm holes in the body piece. Paint the pieces and tape them as shown.

Ask a friend to help you put your outfit on.

Behind you!

Here's another idea for a giant puppet. Tape together several sheets of newspaper. Lie down on the paper and ask a friend to draw around you. This will give you a pattern for cutting your puppet pieces.

Make your puppet pieces larger than your pattern.

The string joints allow you to move the arms around.

Cut the head and top of the body in one piece, the legs and feet in one piece, and the arms in two pieces. Make holes in the cardboard where the pieces join. Poke short, thick cords through the holes and knot the ends. Tape a cardboard handle to the back of the head. Poke long pieces of cord through the hands and knot them on the front. Use the other ends of the long cords to control the arms.

GETTING READY

Here are a few hints and tips that may help when you put on a puppet show for your friends and family.

Posters and invitations

Make sure as many people as possible know about the show well in advance. Make posters giving the time, date, and place of the performance and the name of the show. They should be as bright and colorful as possible. Send invitations to your friends with the same information.

> Don't be afraid to use different kinds of puppets in your show.

A helping hand

People will probably be only too happy to help with the performance. Make sure everyone has a special job and knows when it needs to be done. You may need help with puppet making, setting up the theater, or handing out drinks on the big day. Don't be afraid to ask!

Write it down

Because you'll have so much to remember on the day of your puppet show, it's a good idea to write lists of things to do. Give copies to the friends who are helping you.

There's just enough time for a final run-through—costumes, music, sound effects...

Make sure your puppets are in perfect working order before the show.

I'm sure everything will seem a lot better when I've got my head together.

Instant stage

Not only is this an easy stage to set up, but it will work with all kinds of puppets. Crouch behind the curtain for rod and glove puppets. Stand behind it to operate string puppets in front of the curtain.

29

SHOWTIME

The big day has arrived and the show must go on! Make sure everyone has a seat and that all can see the stage and hear the "puppets" speaking.

Ladies and gentlemen, welcome to the puppet show of the century!

I hope she remembers my lines!

If you're using string puppets, hang them up before you use them so the strings don't get tangled.

DON'T WORRY IF YOU FORGET YOUR WORDS! MAKE SOMETHING UP AND GO WITH IT!

★

DON'T CHOOSE PLAYS WITH TOO MANY WORDS. ON THE WHOLE, PUPPETS ARE BETTER AT DOING THINGS THAN THEY ARE AT TALKING.

★

REMEMBER THAT PUPPETS CAN DO COMPLETELY UNREALISTIC THINGS THAT PEOPLE CAN'T.

Quick change

If you are including different kinds of puppets in your show, use a stage that will adapt easily. The audience will be grateful for a pause between acts, and you will need time to change props and scenery and to make sure that you have the right puppets ready. Announce each act and let the audience settle down before you start. Most important of all, take a big bow at the end of the show!

INDEX

You were great, but now it's back in the box till the next time!